SCIENCE WIDE OPEN
Women in Chemistry

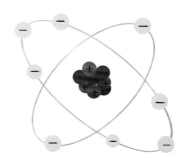

Written by Mary Wissinger
Illustrated by Danielle Pioli

Created and edited by John J. Coveyou

Science, Naturally!
An imprint of Platypus Media, LLC
Washington, D.C.

What is the world made of?

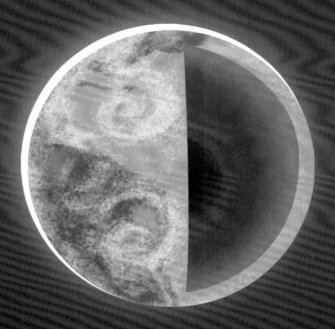

Now that's an awesome question, one that people
have been asking for thousands of years.

Scale

In ancient times, Cleopatra the Alchemist learned about the world by conducting experiments, weighing things, and taking measurements. She was studying matter—that's anything we can weigh and that takes up space.

She also tried to turn ordinary metals into silver or gold. It didn't work, but she was one of the earliest women studying chemistry.

(Egypt, Third or Fourth Century)

7

What is chemistry?

Chemistry is the science of matter and the changes matter goes through. You could also say it's the science of stuff and how it works!

From the air you breathe to the cells in your body, matter and chemistry are everywhere. All the matter in the universe is made up of just three tiny particles: protons, neutrons, and electrons.

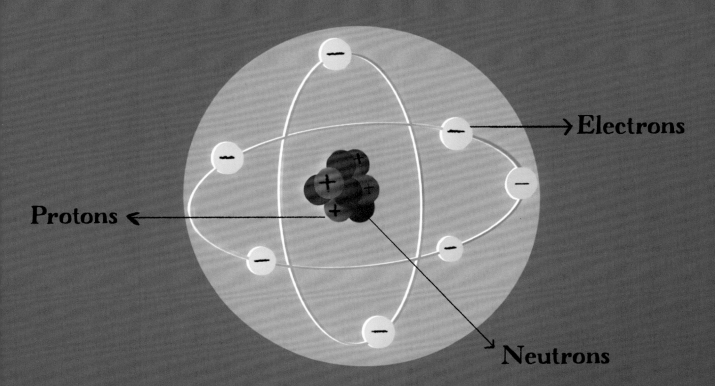

Electrons

Protons

Neutrons

Really? Even me?

Yes! The protons, neutrons, and electrons get together to build many types of atoms. Imagine atoms as the building blocks for everything in the universe.

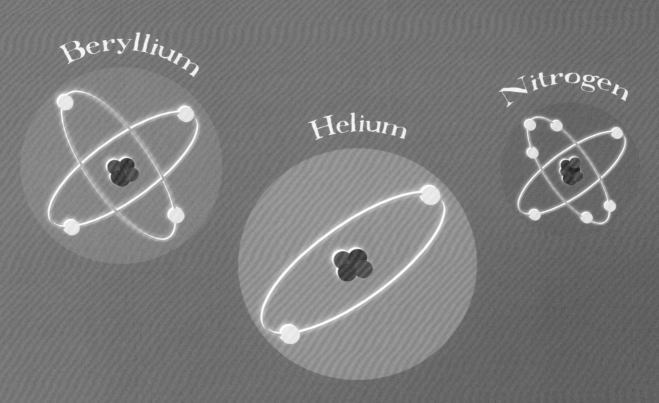

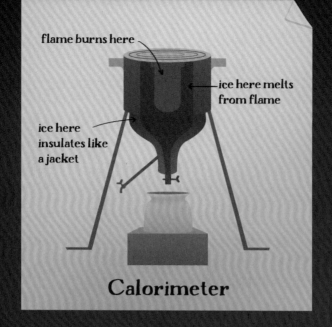

flame burns here

ice here melts
from flame

ice here
insulates like
a jacket

Calorimeter

Groups of the same type of atom are called
elements, and Marie-Anne Paulze Lavoisier
helped write about them in the first modern
chemistry textbook. Her drawings showed
people how chemistry experiments worked.
The book also had a list of elements like oxygen,
hydrogen, and carbon, which are on our periodic
table today.

13

(France, 1758–1836)

What is the periodic table?

The periodic table is the chart that organizes all of the elements.

Just like books in a library have a special place, each element has its own spot and symbol. The elements are lined up by how many protons they've got, and split into columns by how the elements behave.

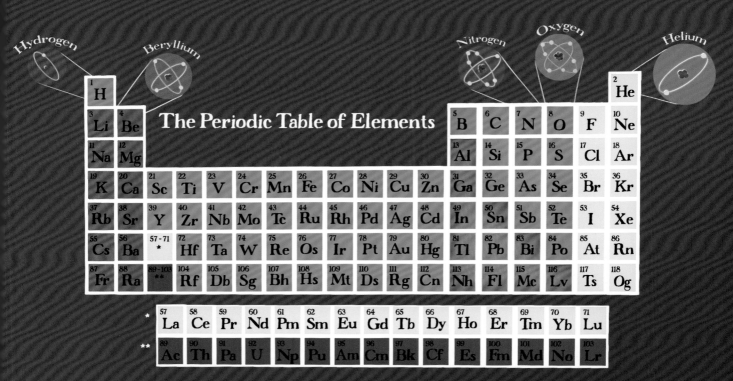

The Periodic Table of Elements

15

Have we discovered every element that could ever exist?

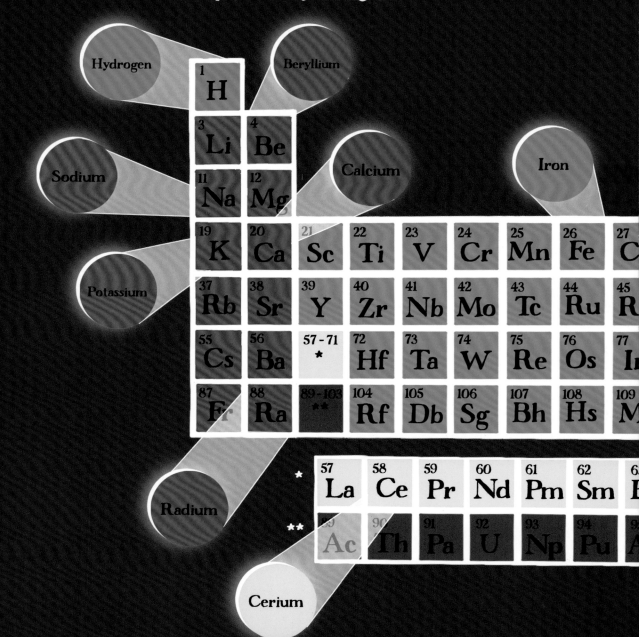

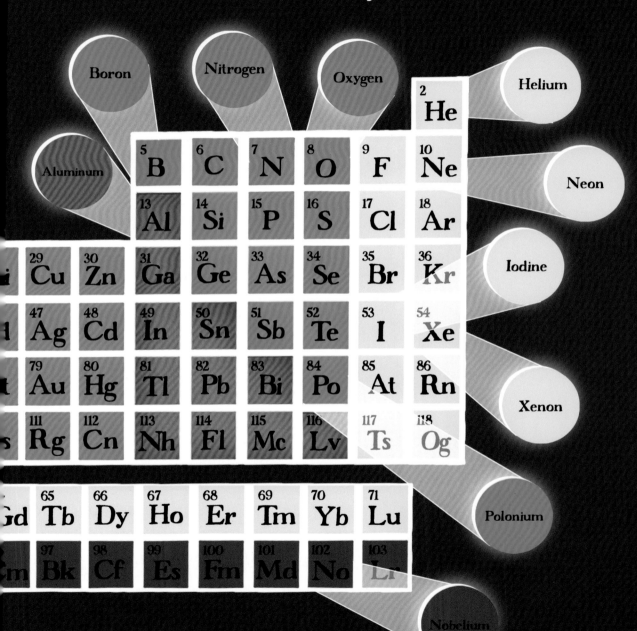

Cyclotron

Dawn Shaughnessy is working to find new ones. She leads a team of scientists that has discovered six new elements so far.

Using a high powered machine called a cyclotron to smash atoms together, she watches to see if the atoms combine to form a new element. These elements haven't been seen before on Earth, and it can take years to prove they exist. Some of them, like livermorium, exists for less than a second! Most elements last longer than that, though.

19

(United States, 1972–)

What elements am I made of?

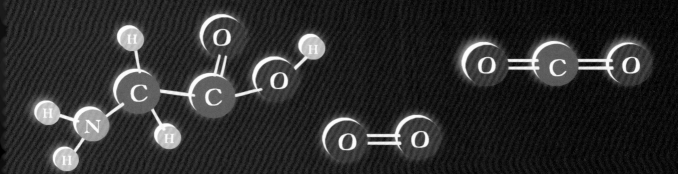

You're made up mostly of oxygen, carbon, hydrogen, nitrogen, calcium, and phosphorus.

They team up to build molecules, which form the structures in your body and go through millions of chemical reactions.

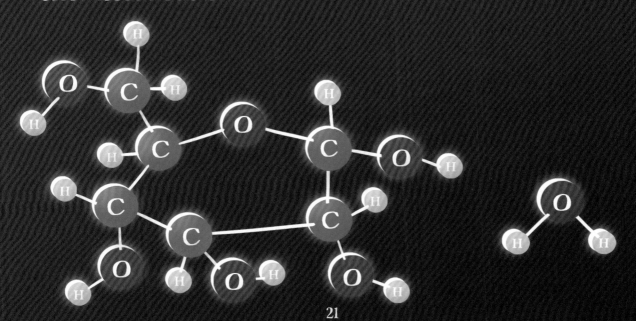

Glucose + $6O_2 \rightarrow 6CO_2 + 6H_2O$ + Energy

Chemical reactions?
What are those?

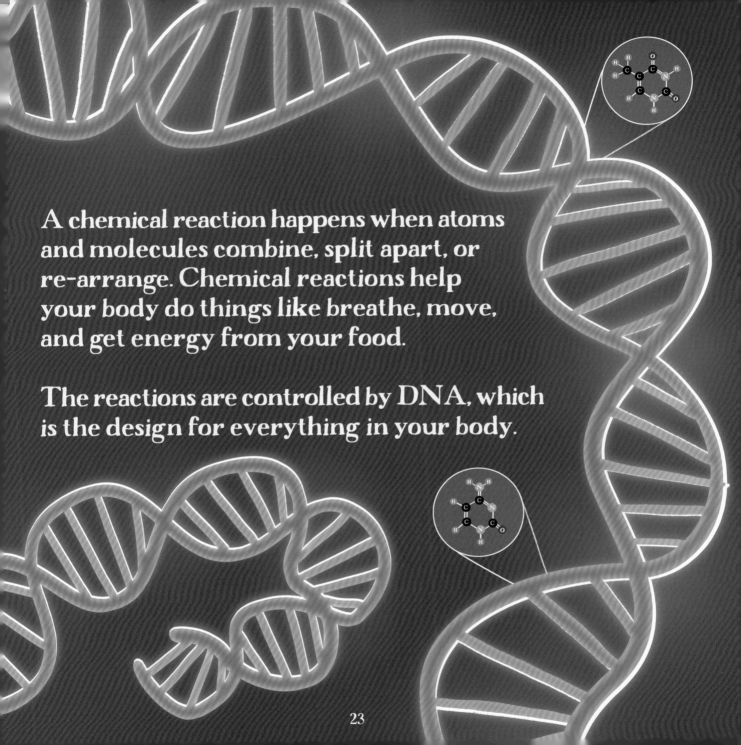

A chemical reaction happens when atoms and molecules combine, split apart, or re-arrange. Chemical reactions help your body do things like breathe, move, and get energy from your food.

The reactions are controlled by DNA, which is the design for everything in your body.

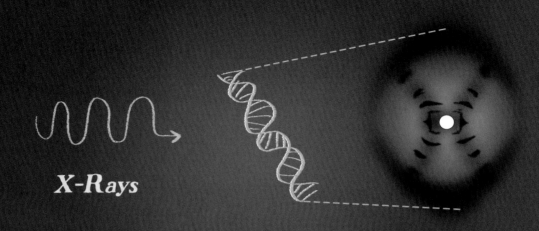

X-Rays

X-Ray Pattern of DNA

DNA is shaped like a twisted ladder called a double helix, but we didn't know what it looked like until Rosalind Franklin. She worked very carefully to take the best pictures of DNA.

Sometimes her pictures took 24 hours before they were ready. Her DNA pictures helped scientists figure out how DNA carries the information that is read by our bodies.

(England, 1920–1958)

How can my body read DNA?

Ada Yonath figured out how our bodies read DNA. She discovered the chemistry and shape of the ribosome, a structure inside our cells. It took her 20 years of experiments and research to figure out how ribosomes work.

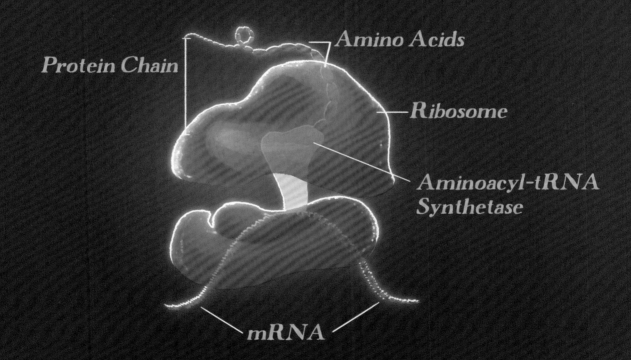

Protein Chain

Amino Acids

Ribosome

Aminoacyl-tRNA Synthetase

mRNA

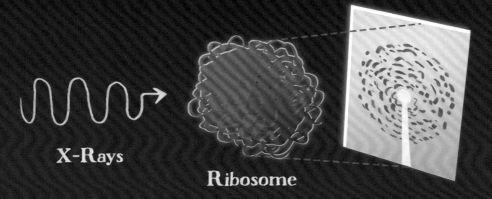

Photographic Plate

X-Rays

Ribosome

Ada studied special cells and used technology called crystallography. She discovered that our bodies make a copy of our DNA instructions, called mRNA. Then one half of the ribosome reads the mRNA instructions, and the other half follows the instructions to make the proteins that build our bodies.

Ada won a Nobel Prize for her work, because it helps explain how all living things—like you—are built!

(Israel, 1939–)

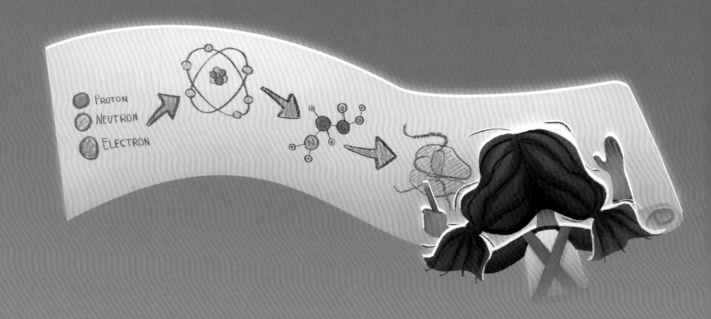

How did she know where to look
for the ribosomes?

Ada was inspired by reading about polar bears. When polar bears hibernate for the winter, their ribosomes pack together and get ready to build proteins in the spring. This idea helped Ada think about the shape of ribosomes, and come up with new ideas for her experiment.

Chemists, like all scientists, are curious and get their inspiration from almost anywhere.

Any time they ask a question, it leads them to the next question.

Like me! I'm already a chemist!

Yes, you are. When you ask a question and look for an answer, you are already a chemist.

And here's the best part:
The whole universe is your experiment!

Can you find...?

Cleopatra the Alchemist (clee-oh-PAT-rah)

Marie-Anne Paulze Lavoisier (mar-EE ann pawls la-vaw-zee-EH)

Dawn Shaughnessy (dawn SHAW-nes-see)

Rosalind Franklin (RAW-za-lind FRANK-lin)

Ada Yonath (AH-dah YON-ah)

Glossary

ALCHEMIST: Someone in ancient times who tried to turn ordinary metals into gold or silver, or find one cure that would work for all sicknesses.

ATOMS: The building blocks that put together our universe. Different kinds of atoms are made by combining different numbers of protons, neutrons, and electrons.

CELLS: The basic structural unit for all organisms. Cells hold the biological equipment to keep an organism alive and successful.

CHEMICAL REACTION: A process where the structure of something, like a molecule, is rearranged.

CHEMICAL STRUCTURE: The way the atoms are arranged in a substance.

CHEMISTRY: The study of matter and the changes that happen to it.

CRYSTALLOGRAPHY: A branch of science that studies the arrangement of atoms in crystals, like salt or diamonds, which are made with strict repeating patterns.

CYCLOTRON: A circular machine that pushes electrically charged particles, like protons, along a spiral path. They are used to bring about high-speed particle collisions.

DNA (Deoxyribonucleic Acid): The written plan in the cells of living things (like plants, animals, and people) that tells each cell, and by extension, the body, how to grow and function.

ELECTRONS: Very teeny particles with a negative electric charge. Electrons travel around the nucleus of every atom.

ELEMENT: A basic substance made of one type of atom that cannot usually be separated into simpler substances.

EXPERIMENT: A test to collect information about the world to see if a hypothesis is correct.

HELIX: A long spiral shape, like a corkscrew or a slinky.

HYPOTHESIS: An educated guess that a person makes to explain something they think is true or will happen.

MASS: A measure of how much matter is in an object. Mass is different from weight because the mass of an object never changes, but its weight will change based on its location in the universe.

MATTER: Anything that takes up space and has mass.

MOLECULE: A group of atoms that are bonded together.

NEUTRONS: Very teeny particles with no electric charge, found in the nucleus of most atoms.

NOBEL PRIZE: A set of very prestigious annual international awards recognizing academic, cultural, and scientific advances. The awards are named for Swedish scientist Alfred Nobel, and were first awarded in 1895.

PERIODIC TABLE: A chart that arranges chemical elements. It is organized by the element's atomic number. The atomic number comes from how many protons the element has.

PROTEINS: Chain-like molecules that are made up of small substances called amino acids. Muscles, organs, and the immune system are mostly made of proteins.

PROTONS: Very teeny particles with a positive electric charge. Protons are in the nucleus of every atom.

RIBOSOMES: Sphere-shaped structures inside a cell that read the cell's mRNA (messenger Ribonucleic Acid) and make proteins.

X-RAY: Invisible waves of energy that can pass through solid objects. X-ray images can show the inside of an object, like a suitcase or a person's body.

Science Wide Open: Women in Chemistry
Copyright © 2022, 2021, 2019, 2016 Genius Games, LLC
Originally published by Genius Games, LLC in 2016

Written by Mary Wissinger
Illustrated by Danielle Pioli
Created and edited by John J. Coveyou

Published by Science, Naturally!
English hardback first edition • 2016 • ISBN: 978-1-945779-10-7
    Second edition • November 2019
English paperback first edition • February 2021 • ISBN: 978-1-938492-31-0
    Second edition • May 2022
English eBook first edition • 2016 • ISBN: 978-1-945779-13-8
    Second edition • November 2019
Spanish paperback first edition • February 2021 • ISBN: 978-1-938492-32-7
Spanish eBook first edition • February 2021 • ISBN: 978-1-938492-33-4

Enjoy all the titles in the series:
    Women in Biology • Las mujeres en la biología
    Women in Chemistry • Las mujeres en la química
    Women in Physics • Las mujeres en la física
    Women in Engineering • Las mujeres en la ingeniería
    Women in Medicine • Las mujeres en la medicina
    Women in Botany • Las mujeres en la botánica

Teacher's Guide available at the Educational Resources page of ScienceNaturally.com.

Published in the United States by:
    Science, Naturally!
        An imprint of Platypus Media, LLC
    750 First Street, NE, Suite 700
    Washington, DC 20002
    202-465-4798 • Fax: 202-558-2132
    Info@ScienceNaturally.com • ScienceNaturally.com

Distributed to the trade by:
    National Book Network (North America)
        301-459-3366 • Toll-free: 800-462-6420
        CustomerCare@NBNbooks.com • NBNbooks.com
    NBN international (worldwide)
        NBNi.Cservs@IngramContent.com • Distribution.NBNi.co.uk

Library of Congress Control Number: 2020020303

11 10 9 8 7 6 5 4 3 2

Printed in China